MW01154210

God Hears You

Authored by God

Written by
Lucy W. Kernodle

Laine N. Francis
Artist

ISBN 978-1-63961-425-7 (hardcover)
ISBN 978-1-63961-424-0 (digital)

Christian Faith Publishing
832 Park Avenue
Meadville, PA 16335
www.christianfaithpublishing.com

Printed in the United States of America

A true story, authored by God,
and written prayerfully to
nourish the young hearts for
which it was intended.

For my husband
and our eldest son
his father's namesake,
Donald Reed Kernodle Jr.
Both of whom are in heaven.

When you tumble ashore
All broken and spent
To the feet of God
He will fix you, stretch out His merciful hand,
Make you whole again—
To fly once more, as you were intended.

Unknown

This is a story about a girl named Lucy, that's me, and a seagull named 64439171. It is a true story. A miracle story that really did happen. Promise!

You see, I was walking down the beach late one afternoon after everyone had gone back to their homes from a day of sand and water fun. Alone I was, just taking a stroll toward the end of the island where the channel separates one island from the next. As the beach narrowed, I could see the ocean on my left and just over the sand dunes, directly to my right, was the sound or the inland waterway. It was oh so beautiful and quiet. Just me, Lucy. No people, no houses, no one in sight—anywhere!

Suddenly I started hearing lots and lots of commotion (that means noise) coming from two seagulls as they flew very short distances from one sand dune to the next. They would start to fly and then quickly drop down, I guessed, to take a rest. All the while they were loudly squawking and squawking. (That's what seagulls do—squawk.)

Well, there must be something wrong, I thought.

I'll just run up really fast and see what's the matter. But every time I tried to run up close, they would quickly fly ahead to still another sand dune.

Oh my! I did this about three times, and it made me really, really tired, all that running fast uphill in the deep sand. I did get close enough to see that one of the gulls was hampered (that means slowed down) by something holding his foot and tail together. So that was why he had a hard time flying happily.

Oh, if only I could catch that bird and see how I could help! Well, you know that was not going to happen. First of all, I could not run as fast as they could fly away from me, and I was sure they were really, really scared of me. Don't you know they were? It was then I became their "brother in arms." (That means to join another in his tough time—as a buddy.)

So I said a prayer. This is what I prayed:

> "Dear God, *if you would help me catch that poor bird, I just know I could free him.*"

By now I had walked to the very end of the island. I never took my eyes off the two birds, never. I was right where the dunes and the beach met the channel. I stood and watched them fly straight over the narrow channel away from me to the next island. I was so sad they were leaving, and I didn't get a chance to help.

Well, to my amazement, they took a sharp left turn over to the ocean, way out in front of where I was standing. I never, not ever, had taken another step. I just turned my feet when their direction changed.

All of a sudden one bird fell right down to the water. I guessed he was the one tangled up, and he must have been all tired out. He floated there, about fifty yards in front of me (that's about half of a football field). I could see the strong waves crashing over him as he was getting tossed about. It made me so unhappy not even being able to help him. It was, however, a lovely sight to see his mate staying close by, hovering over him (that means remaining in one place in the air), still squawking! Now a group of nine seagulls came directly over him. They were swooping down in rapid succession, one at a time. It seemed they were imploring him (that means begging) to fly. They stayed just a few minutes, and before I knew it, they were gone.

Now there was only one gull in the water and his mate flying above, still squawking with her encouragement. It was as if he was hearing, "Don't give up. Don't give up." I watched sadly as the breaking waves were tumbling him about, and he could no longer help himself.

Soon as the waves neared the shore, they calmed down. I was surprised to see him coming closer and closer to where I was standing. I was so proud to see his faithful mate still squawking just overhead, lending her support by her presence. I was absolutely transfixed (that means spellbound). I could not believe what was happening right before my eyes. I did not move. Not even one inch! He was coming straight toward me with the now soft waves pushing him gently forward. Gosh, he came so close I could have dashed out and grabbed him up, but I was powerless to move. Frozen! How could this be happening?

Now he was so close—right in front of me. He was much bigger than he had looked flying in the air—*big* like a Thanksgiving turkey! My feet were still planted in the sand with space between them. He drifted right up between my feet. Yes, he did! Can you believe it?

As I leaned over to pick him up and check out his injury, he pecked at me really hard and I knew we had a problem.

Oh, if only someone could be here to help us. I did see his tail was all tangled in a mess of fishing line—yes, fishing line. And his poor foot had a fishhook in it. I bet that really hurt! That's why he couldn't fly. Oh my, what to do?

It would surely take more than just my two hands to free him. I needed two hands to hold his beak from biting and two hands to untangle him. You remember I was all alone on the far end of the island, don't you?

Well, I stood and turned around in desperation (that means not knowing what to do). There, to my great surprise, was a woman with long black hair sitting on an Indian blanket only a few yards behind me. I didn't have time to think about where she had come from or how long she had been there. The seagull needed help in a hurry! I quickly picked up the gull from the back, as I had learned my lesson earlier. I ran up to her and asked if she would please hold him securely so I could free him. I worked as quickly as I could. He was, oh, so upset! Would you be surprised if I told you that his mate was now hovering (you remember what that means?) right over our heads? She squawked as we worked really fast! The woman never said a word.

AVISE BI
WRITE WAS.
USA
64439171

While untangling him, I noticed he was a banded bird. That is when birds are given a bracelet with a number so good people who are interested in helping birds can trace where they travel and where they build their new homes. Of course, you guessed it, his band had the number 64439171 on it! How about that? I was so excited! My heart was thumping hard inside my chest.

I took him from the woman's hold, ran directly in back of her, toward the dunes, and threw him up toward the sky.

"Thank you, God. Oh, thank you!" That's what I said as I stood there watching him fly with his mate over the dunes and into the evening sky. There was suddenly no more squawking.

What a miracle! What a miracle!

I watched thankfully as they disappeared from sight, then I turned around, talking really fast about what just happened…and *what*? Why, the lady was gone! She was nowhere… nowhere. There were no houses nearby that she could have walked to on the far end of the island. I saw no boat to carry her away, and she surely wasn't swimming! She had never spoken a word to me, and now she was gone, just like the two seagulls.

I didn't even get to thank her, I sadly thought.

It was then that I realized the woman was an angel sent by God. He cared for that seagull in pain. He used me and an angel to free him. Just think how much more God cares for us when we get all tangled up in our lives. He is there for us, hears our prayers, and sends help because He loves us and all the wonderful creatures He has made.

I have never forgotten that beautiful day. I never will.

God hears you!

Look at the birds of the air.
They don't plant or gather crops.
They don't put away crops in storerooms.
But your Father who is in heaven feeds them.
Aren't you worth much more than they are?

—Matthew 6:26 (NIRV)

Did You Know?

This true story about me, Lucy, and 64439171 is a miracle story. I later researched his band number and found out he was banded in Virginia, flew all the way down the coast of North Carolina, and I met him on the beach of Litchfield, South Carolina (that's over 350 miles). He and his mate had really done some flying, don't you think?

What about this story now? I believe in miracles, and I know God answers prayers, even for the birds. How much more does He care for you and me? He is touched by those in distress—whether they are people, birds, or other animals. He sends love to rescue those in trouble. I thank God for this lesson of love and pray I never forget. I wonder what it does inside your heart as you read it?

Maybe, just maybe, the next time you go to the beach, you might see 64439171's bright band flashing in the sun as he goes by. While it may not be a seagull, you can always be ready when God needs you to help the one He loves—and that means people too! God's plan is to save us all.

This is a picture of his bird band.

Let's Talk about It

What do you think the meaning of this story is? What was your favorite part?

When Lucy prayed for God's help, she knew she would be unable to free 64439171 all by herself. Who did God send that day?

Do we always know when God saves us? Can angels be disguised in other ways to help God?

Have you ever been able to help someone in trouble?

Do you think it was God's plan to use the seagulls, Lucy, and the woman in this miracle rescue?

What gift did Lucy and 64439171 share?

How did Lucy feel when she realized God had heard her prayer for help?

You too can be a part of God's rescue plan as we listen and watch carefully for his directions.

One precious prayer, in childlike faith, was heard above

The unexpected answer drifted up between my feet!

About the Author

Lucy W. Kernodle lives in Burlington, North Carolina, where she and her husband raised five children. Her writing personal imaginary stories have been a true delight for each of their thirteen grandchildren. She has been honored, for many years, to incorporate her love for children and with her past training of BSN, RN, as a patient-care volunteer for both adults and children in Hospice Care.